# What others are saying

"Not only a great story, but also a guide to becoming a better leader of others and yourself. Full of solid lessons and valuable reminders that forces you to pay attention to your own habits and relationships."

**J. Berg**, VP Sales Manager

"Laurie-Ann shows a set of tools for anyone who works with people. This is about becoming a better leader, and a better person. You'll use it at work and in your personal life. Read it! You'll buy it for others."

**Andrea G.**, Hotel General Manager

"Don't be fooled by the simplicity of her message. Laurie-Ann provides yet another powerful message with practical real-life solutions to improve your leadership skills. Anyone wanting to have a bigger impact needs to read this book."

**Peter Boyle**, CEO **IdeaPoC.com**

"Without lecturing, Laurie-Ann lets us experience firsthand remarkable leadership. Her story celebrates the skill of coaching and it connects perfectly with our familiar day-to-day business."

**Sven Gade**, CEO of LeaderTrip Coaching
LeaderTrip-Coaching.com

"Rethink Your Leadership opened my eyes to a new way of leading: how I impact those that I lead, and how to leave a legacy. It took me out of the realm of "if this/then that" type of leadership. The story format make the challenges and difficulties of management instantly relatable. I kept finding my self thinking "I've been there" as I read through the book. The idea of leaving a legacy and actually impacting those under your supervision is something that is so often neglected in today's "just get it done," and "numbers" focused businesses. If I'm not remembered but left a positive impact, I will have been successful. I loved the book. "

**J. Maguire**, Regional Manager

"Leadership books are everywhere and most come and go rapidly. Not Laurie-Ann! Laurie-Ann Murabito doesn't go away rapidly and she makes her personal lessons-based readings last! This book has real heart and soul, and the inspiring story is one that all professionals will relate to. She knows organizations don't do great things...smart, talented, leaders do!"

**Lawrence A. Colby**
Author of "The Devil Dragon Pilot", CEO of Mach278

# Rethink Your Leadership

*Influence Your Team to Empower and Promote Engagement*

By
Laurie-Ann Murabito

ISBN: 1540610934
ISBN 13: 978-1540610935

# Dedication

This book is dedicated to some close friends, who gently encouraged and frequently asked me how the book was coming along. Thank you Emy Hoff, Jeremy Berg, Peter Boyle, Jon Sweatman and Andrea and Sven Gade. Thank you to my favorite barista, Danielle for your smile and hot coffee to start the writing experience each day. To my editor, Lisa Schleipfer, whose talents make my words come to life and to Bonnie Robert's keen eye for detail.

And to my husband, Michael, thank you for your love, support, encouragement and making me laugh every single day.

# Introduction

Thank you for purchasing *Rethink Your Leadership*. This book is a modern day parable, to reveal and look at your leadership as a journey. I have learned, both with helping my clients and during my own leadership journey, that it *is* a journey. Outstanding leaders are constantly learning, critiquing, developing, and creating their own unique style of leadership. And with that comes a plan for development.

The reason I wrote this book was because I got hundreds of questions after my first book, *Rethink Leadership: Four Lessons to Make You Remarkable*. The questions varied from *How do I get from where I am today to the next level? What do I need to do to get that next promotion? How do I begin to discover my own style of leadership? What makes a good leader?*—the list goes on.

In working with a number of private one-on-one executive clients—and also audiences—having spoken to thousands of people, all searching for the answers, one of the things that I have learned through my work with leadership is that leadership is a process

Leadership is not something that you learn once in a book and then you start applying it perfectly right away.

Leadership is constantly changing. The teams that you'll work with will change. The circumstances that you are leading will constantly be changing, and so therefore, your leadership skills will constantly be evolving. You may only use a few skills one day and need to pull out something different from your toolbox the next day.

But I do believe that we all develop a style. We all have a unique style of leadership, and being able to determine that and even decide on what kind of style that you want—will help you along your leadership journey.

There are some things that we are just naturally gifted at. For example, you might be very inspiring with words, while a fellow colleague or another leader might be gifted with stories, and somebody else might be talented at mentoring others. Being able to find out what your strengths are, and using them, is the starting point to your development as an outstanding leader.

This book has been written in a way that it's short, sweet, and to the point. I believe that we all want to grasp the needed information, utilize it quickly, and actually apply it to our lives. Some of the skills that I feel are really important in becoming the best leader are: listening, trust, integrity, how you communicate with your team, and leading up. One of the basic things that we're going to start with is how to define leadership.

At the end of each chapter, there are a few thought provoking questions for you and space to write your answers. These questions are to help you deepen your learning as you move through this book.

I hope you enjoy this modern-day exchange between two people. Sit back, grab a cup of coffee or a mug of tea, and enjoy the story. At the end of each chapter are questions for you to think about and then write down your answers. Please take the time to answer them right away. This book was meant as a gift to guide you along your journey, and become the best leader that you can possibly be.

As always, be remarkable,

*Laurie-Ann*

*There is no such thing as an accident; it is fate misnamed.*

**-Napoleon Bonaparte**

# Chapter 1: A Chance Meeting

Alan steps off the elevator, briefcase in one hand and smartphone in the other, using his thumb to glance and flip through e-mails. Ah, the morning ritual to determine which e-mails he needs to respond to first when he arrives at his desk. Walking down the hallway, with his head down, he walks the familiar pathway to his office. Occasionally, his eyes glance up from his phone, momentarily to ensure his safety and for others. He hears a number of voices say, "Good morning, Alan," but he barely responds with anything more than a half smile.

Walking past Mary, he utters his first incomprehensible words. Mary smirks and follows him with her eyes to his office where he drops his briefcase down on his desk with a loud thud. He takes a deep breath, followed by a long exhale, getting ready for another week.

Mary counts to ten, rises, and walks into his office. Mary is a robust African American woman in her late 40s, who is always impeccably dressed and early to work with her bright smile. You always know where you stand with her; she never keeps her opinions to herself. You either love her or hate her for that, but she's honest, consistent, and has your back.

"Morning. You look terrible."

"Thanks, do I pay you to say that?"

"No, free of charge. And may I remind you, you don't pay me, that's payroll's job. If you did, I would demand a raise, a great BIG raise," she says with a glimmer of sarcasm. "Another sleepless night?"

"I got some, but not enough."

She plops down one of two piles of folders she's holding. One is significantly higher than the other. "These are the emergencies ... things that need your attention now," and then she puts down a lighter set of folders. "These are the things that need your attention, but not today."

Alan looks at the difference in the piles. "Why is the emergency pile so much bigger than the other pile? It's the same every week. Mary, can you please explain that to me?"

"Happy Monday." Smiling, she pivots on her heel and walks out of the office. Alan is left sitting there shaking his head. It's only been a few months since he received this promotion and it's not what he expected. It's not what he interviewed for, nor were they forthcoming with all of the real problems that this department was having. He asked all the right questions and observed the best he could. Then again, he might not have noticed the warning signs, as he knew this would be the right move for his career in the long run. He can't remember the last good night sleep he had.

Mary returns, "Oh, and here's your schedule for today and the week, a list of your meetings and top priorities. I rescheduled a couple of your non-urgent meetings to free up time in your schedule to attend to those emergencies."

"Thanks, Mary, as always, you keep me on track. I really appreciate it."

He skims through the list of meetings; one problem after another, which needs his attention and solutions. He needs to hire two people for openings he has, "I don't even know whether I'm going to have time to do that on top of all these other meetings and planning committees that need my attention as well." Alan takes a deep breath while he shakes his head.

Later that day, Alan is walking out of a meeting room, while summarizing with one of the other department managers. Smiling and nodding, to make it look like he's got everything under control. Instead, he's thinking about his dysfunctional team, the daily growing problem list, and about the expectations of those who promoted him.

This new division is extremely demanding and he doesn't want to let anybody down. He is the right choice for this position and it's a great strategic career move. But all he can think about is, "I feel like I'm drowning. I can't seem to tread water long enough to make a difference. I feel like I'm constantly putting out fires." Coming from the patient care side of healthcare should have-in theory- prepared him for the commercial side of healthcare.

Looking down at his phone as he's heading towards the elevator Alan sees a familiar face in the distance. That distinct smile of an old friend, someone he admires and respects. The person Alan learned so much from, when he worked for him in his earlier career days. "Jack! How are you?"

Jack extends his arm, "Alan, how are you? What a nice surprise to run into you."

"It's really nice to run into you, too. Where are you these days?"

"I'm working with some of my favorite clients. I've become a consultant working for myself. The skills that I learned in leadership and team development has helped me in sales and consulting. How have you been? I heard that you got a very nice promotion."

"Yes, I did. I've been there for about … a couple of months now."

"How is it going?"

Alan pauses with his answer, which is a dead give away to Jack. "Okay … it's going well."

"Really? Is it really going well or were you up late watching the game? You look a little tired."

"Well, Jack, to be honest with you, I did watch the game last night. It started off great with two touchdowns in the first quarter, but then they caught up. It was nerve wracking."

"I was up late too watching them. That last Hail Mary. Wow!"

"But football isn't why I look tired. The new position is a little more challenging than I had anticipated. There are a lot of demands and meetings, not to mention the problems that need to be solved. That's what they're expecting me to do–solve them."

"How is your team?"

"The team? You know … they're okay. I do have a couple of openings to fill. I'm just not quite sure when I'm going to have time to interview for those positions. HR has sent up a number of resumes with their suggestions."

"Well, Alan, let me suggest you hire the right person for each of those positions, and don't just hire a warm body."

"What do you mean by that?"

"Well, I have learned a few things, through my years—and I do have a few more years on you—early in my career I made this very mistake. We hire a resume instead of hiring a personality. You want to make sure, always make sure, you hire the right person, for not only the position but for the culture of your department or company."

"It sounds like some good advice, but honestly I'm not sure I have that much time, to wait for that right person."

"If you don't take the time now, it will cost you in the end. And it will cost you a whole lot more in time wasted in training, recruiting again, the legal issues and time associated with getting rid of someone who doesn't fit, just to name a few."

"Okay, well when you put it that way. Um, is there any chance that maybe the two of us could sit down and have coffee? Or meet for lunch?"

"Yeah, let's do that. Tell you what, have Mary call me and we'll put something on our calendars. We'll get that booked as soon as possible."

"That sounds great. Thanks, Jack. Have a great day."

"Have a great day yourself."

"Wait, Jack ... ah ... how did you know Mary's name?"

Jack smiles, "I keep a watchful eye on certain people who worked with me, and you're one of them. See you soon."

Alan watches as Jack walks down the hall, flattered he was one of the people he'd kept an eye on from afar. He feels a sense of relief, knowing he might be able to pick Jack's brain and tap into his experience. He always admired him, not because he had done extremely well throughout his career, but because of who he is as a person. Jack was a great leader; somebody to learn from.

"He doesn't know what an impact he has had on my life," Alan mumbles to himself. "I took away from him what I needed back then. Today, I'm in a different place, and I will be the student again with Jack as my teacher. I wonder if he has room to mentor and coach me again?"

## Questions:

- Who has had an impact on your career or life?

- What are you tired of doing or what frustrates you? What are you ready to change?

- How would you like to grow and improve your impact on others?

*Start by doing what's necessary; then do what's possible; and suddenly you are doing the impossible.*

**-Francis of Assisi**

# Chapter 2: The Luncheon

The day arrives for the anticipated lunch meeting; a new sandwich lunch spot not too far from Alan's office.

Alan arrives rushing, grabs his seat quickly, "Hey, Jack. Sorry I'm late." He places his briefcase off to the side of his chair as he catches his breath.

Jack nods and places the portfolio he's reviewing down by his side.

Alan nodding, "Yah ... I remember what you used to say and teach us about being on time, if not early. This new position really eats away at my time. I feel I'm always late these days."

"We're old friends, let's not dwell on it. Tell me about what's going on. Why did you want to talk?"

"Honestly, Jack, and this is just between the two of us, I feel like I'm drowning. I feel like there are more problems and issues that need my immediate attention. Every day I discover more issues than need to be to solve. And, I know, I mentioned to you that I need to hire some new people, and I don't know when I'm going to have time to do that, not with all these meetings, headaches and fires to put out. The list goes on."

"What can I help you with? What would benefit you today, right now?"

"I've been thinking about that, for the past couple of days. You were a great mentor years ago, when I was just starting out in my career. I was wondering if you would be open to being my mentor again, but different."

"How different?"

"I need different help than I did previously because now I'm responsible for more people than I ever was in my past. You gave me a number of skills and shared advice that served me professionally. You taught me things that I didn't learn in college or from other positions. I was ready to learn them, when you were, my boss. You taught—not just me, but all of us—about communications skills, the importance of body language, the power of rapport and influence, all the way down to how dress for the various occasions we found ourselves in."
breath in before continuing, "Would you help me with leadership skills? I want to become the kind of leader that not only helps my company but the people I'm leading. What do I need to know? How can I lead this team more effectively?"

"Well, Alan, that's a big order. First of all, it's not something we're going to finish in one luncheon or that you'll achieve in one month. It has taken me years to learn, understand, and develop my own leadership style. As a matter of fact, I consider leadership to be an art form. No artist is ever completely done mastering their craft or finished learning about the different mediums they use. They're constantly learning. So as a leader, this is something you will need to commit to. A promise to yourself. The reasons and people that you'll lead will vary. Let's start with your department. Tell me about your team, the people you work with."

"My team," Alan smirks and subconsciously rolls his eyes, "is mostly un-ambitious. All are college educated and between their late 20s to mid 40s. Mary, my assistant, I'm guessing she's older than me. She keeps me focused. There's a total of ten, and Mary, a mixture of men and women. They look like the walking dead on Monday mornings—okay, most mornings. Not much gets done in the morning hours, and I never schedule meetings until late morning or early afternoon. What else can I tell you?"

"Do you trust them?"

"I wouldn't trust them on their own."

"Why?"

"Because, I see the ball getting dropped too often, there is no hint of them being true to their word. Deadlines get missed. I hear excuses, typically blaming other departments or the client themselves."

"You don't hold them accountable?"

"Jack, I try. I really am trying but they ... it's almost like the culture of this department is not to finish things, where projects and deals go to die."

"Alan, what you have is an engagement problem, or a lack there of."

"What do you mean?"

"Studies report that employee disengagement cost companies a great deal of lost revenue. I'm talking in the hundreds of billions of dollars here in the US alone. Roughly, 85 percent of the working population is some degree of disengagement. That percentage includes managers and leadership, not only front line workers. That means only 15 percent of the workforce is actively engaged in their work."

"Wow. I think all of my team is part of that 85 percent. Mary's my 15 percent."

"Since they've been doing studies on engagement, those percentages have not changed in 20-plus years. I believe that means there is an underlying leadership problem."

"Huh?"

"If you have a safety problem, you have a leadership problem. If you have sales problems, you have a leadership problem. If you have problems with your products, you have a leadership problem. Think back to your days in the hospital environment, the patient care side of healthcare. The people you were leading; if there was a problem of any kind, it was a leadership problem, your problem. Leadership is responsible for setting the tone or the culture of the organization or department. Leaders have more of an impact on engagement than they realize. Better engagement, leads to better sales, safety, patient care, customer satisfaction, loyalty, innovation, products, etc. There's another side to engagement too; the employees perspective. Better engagement levels create improved job satisfaction, performance, loyalty and decreasing attrition rates."

"Okay, I guess the next question I have is: How can I put life back into my team? How do I improve the engagement?"

"Glad you asked. You'll have to develop your own unique style of leadership."

"My own unique leadership style? Is there a book I should read or listen to during my commute?"

"Yes, Alan, there are a number of different books that you can read. As a matter of fact, I'll have one sent over to your office. It's a quick read, and you'll enjoy it. Reading is only part of what you need to do to become a great leader. You'll also have to put what you learn into action, what I share with you and what you learn from reading. Reading is great, but it's when you put the lessons into action that makes the difference. Also, you'll need to do some soul searching."

Lifting up the menu Jack continued, "But let's look at the menu first. I don't know about you, Alan, but I'm hungry."

After the waitress had stepped away from the table with their orders, Jack continued, "Alan, pull out some paper and a pen. I want you to think about two or three people in your past who were awful managers, terrible leaders. They could have been people that you worked for as a volunteer at a non profit, maybe a part-time job when you were in college, or even currently work for. I want you to think of two or three people and write down their names."

Grabbing a pen from the inside of his jacket, Alan starts to write his answers down but pauses. Looking up, "No one is going to see this, right?"

"Nobody is going to see it. Just use initials, as long as you know who they are." Alan continues and looks up when he's done writing down three initials.

"Next, write down four to five characteristics about each of those people that you feel made them bad leaders."

Alan writes down his answers.

"We'll go back to that afterwards. What do you think leadership is?"

A smile grows on Alan's face, as he tilts his head to the left and answers. "Leadership should be inspiring, motivating, even when it's constantly changing. A leader should be growing. It's not always easy ... it's about service ... being of service to somebody else, being of service to the group, the company, the cause, et cetera."

"Great. Now, what I want you to do is write down and think of two to three people whose leadership you admired. Leaders that you flourished under. Again, I want you to do the same thing and write down four to five characteristics about each of them that you admired, that you believed, in your opinion, made them great leaders."

"So let's discuss your answers, start with the negative characteristics first before we move on to the positives."

Alan says, "One of them didn't communicate effectively at all. This leader, which will remain anonymous, barked out commands. Somebody else was extremely intimidating, threatening almost, and never smiled. I and the rest of the team I worked with, never felt like we were on solid ground. Too much uncertainty or a lack of security. In general, I didn't find them to be easy or inspiring leaders to work for."

Jack says, "Tell me how the team reacted? What was it like to work on this team with this style of uninspiring leadership?"

"Um, it was not cooperative. In hindsight, I don't feel like we were able to give it our all, but I do believe we felt like we were giving all that we had at the time. It was an extremely stressful environment and I found it difficult to be creative with problem solving. Our turnover rate was pretty high. We always had someone new on the team to bring up-to-date and train. Ya know, we were told this was a department with turnover because of the stressful nature of our work. And that most were not cut out for this type of work or stress. But, looking back at it, it was the leadership that set the stressful environment or the tone of the department ... wow," Alan pauses before continuing with his thoughts, "Ya know, I never really thought about how bad or uninspiring leadership really does impact the results and productivity of a team."

"Good, let's move onto the positives ones. Tell me about some of the positive characteristics that you wrote down."

A smile came across Alan's face and he sat a little bit taller, "Well, let's see, you mentored and coached us, not just me but everybody that was on our team."

"Thank you. That's very kind of you, Alan. I'm flattered that I was one of those leaders that has impacted you. Who else?"

"Somebody else, I always felt that she was completely supportive and fully present. When I say present, I mean, she was there. She not only had an open-door policy but never rushed us when we needed to discuss a problem or a solution I or we had. I'm saying 'we' because I'm kind of speaking for the group. Another answer that I put down was 'trust.' I wrote down *great listeners, sense of humor, transparent* and *open*.

"Somebody else, I remember always regularly checked in and offered assistance. Another answer is *an ability to bring out the best in us*. I remember someone that I worked for helping me develop skills that I didn't even know I had. He communicated really well, in an encouraging and caring manner. He also had this sense for what somebody needed or he anticipated needs really well. And *respect*; all of these great leaders made me feel respected and that I was a valuable part of the team."

"Great, great, those are some great words, great characteristics. Now, before we leave, I want to give you something to think about. These characteristics obviously resonated with you for a reason. Now, think about these words, the positive and negative and what style of leadership you want to develop. Remember, this is a lifelong process, and I want you to really think about the sort of leader that you want to become. It doesn't take a lifetime to become a good leader. Outstanding leaders never stop learning—about themselves, or about others, or how to lead with impact. Get a journal and write your thoughts and answers in it. There's a reason why I want you to write it down versus typing it to into a computer or just making mental notes. Will you do that for me, Alan?"

"Yes, absolutely."

"Great. I'm sorry I don't have more time to continue discussing this, but as I mentioned earlier, this is not a simple luncheon meeting. This is a process and I want to give you bite-size chunks to work on. So what I want you to do—"

"Are you giving me homework?"

"Well, you could call it homework, if you'd like. I want you to decide on what kind of a leader that you want to become or be known for. So think of it as the legacy you leave behind. The people that you're leading, how do you want them to describe you? Because if there is one thing that I have learned in my career, if you don't decide how you want to be remembered, then somebody else will decide for you. Don't leave it to chance."

"Wow, that's powerful and very true. I never thought of that."

Heading out the door and onto the sidewalk, they finish up their good-byes with a handshake. "Alan, I'll have that book sent over to you, and we'll meet in a couple of weeks."

"Jack, one more thing; it was great seeing you. Thank you very much. I found this extremely helpful so far."

"Alan, we haven't even begun. If you enjoyed this, then you're really going to enjoy what's further down the road from here. See you soon." The two men head off in opposite directions. Alan's mind is spinning, but a weight has been lifted from his shoulders.

Back in his office, he greets Mary as he walks by her workspace. Grabbing his seat behind his large, wooden desk, he spins around to look out the window. The city skyline is stunning with the clear, blue skies in the background. Not a bad perk. He replays his lunch conversation, glancing at the piece of paper he wrote his answers on. He stares at the list of characteristics. Who was he becoming? At the rate he was going, before his lunch, he was headed down the highway of destruction and distraction. Work is consuming of all his thoughts and energy. His wife and kids are feeling neglected, with the promise that *next week things will get better and we'll do things as a family*. Now that he had taken this promotion, time with the family had become rare. Dinner with the family had become an occasional event, maybe twice a week.

The advice from Jack gets him to start thinking about who he wants to become. When he worked for Jack years ago, he experienced what good leadership could be like. What happened since he left the guidance of his leadership? Bad and mediocre leadership seemed to be the norm, and unfortunately, he had picked up bad habits from the wrong role models without even realizing it. His leadership muscle had atrophied or weakened. He'd given up, waved the white flag, given in to the wrong style of leadership, without even knowing it.

*Things will be different.*

Alan makes a decision to draw a line in the sand. He turns back around to face his desk, opens up the bottom left drawer and pulls out a notebook. It now will become his journal. He pulls out the pen from his jacket pocket, dates the top page and begins.

# Questions:

- List 5 characteristics that best describe your current leadership style?

- Think back on someone's leadership you flourished under. List 3 to 5 qualities about their leadership that resonates with you.

- Think back on your past when you worked under poor leadership. List 3 to 5 qualities about their leadership.

*Train people well enough so they can leave, treat them well enough so they don't want to.*"

**-Richard Branson**

# Chapter 3: The Real Goal

Alan waits eagerly, with his journal to his left on the white linen tablecloth. Picking up the ice-cold water glass, he wonders what Jack will share today. He intentionally arrived fifteen minutes early. As a matter of fact, since their last meeting, he vowed to be on time—if not early—for every meeting or appointment that was in his calendar. Looking back, he noticed how his stress level had decreased by being prepared and early for each appointment. When he was less stressed, he was able to be more present in the moment, which made him feel more productive.

Meandering through the dining room, with a smile on his face, Jack arrives.

"Alan, how are you today?" Alan rises to greet his friend and mentor. The two shake hands and take their seats. They discuss the recent sport games and a future business trip before ordering lunch.

Alan shares what he has learned going through the process of focusing on the characteristics of leadership. He includes his observations of other leaders: above, lateral, and below him. He noticed a similarity in the leaders, and it correlates with the in-house leadership development that was fair at best. Alan went through the same day-and half-long process. Certainly, not enough time to teach something as important and impactful as leadership.

Putting down his fork Alan says, "Thank you for the book, Rethink Leadership, you sent over. I really enjoyed it. The modern day parable made it entertaining to learn the powerful, yet simplistic lessons of the book."

"I heard the author at a conference I attended. She was the closing keynote speaker with a very impactful message. And, it's simple, but easily forgotten and overlooked, as we human beings can get sucked into a pattern that is unfulfilling and produces mediocre results. I enjoyed the book so much, I bought a number of copies to give out to those I think would benefit from the message. Whenever my inventory gets low, I reorder."

"Thank you. I actually went online and ordered a few copies for those on my team too. I think my favorite lesson, if I had to pick only one, is about how to raise your bar. But all the lessons are valuable."

"I'm glad you liked that one because that is exactly what you are doing: raising your bar. Today, I thought I would share with you the purpose of the game, and the game is leadership. I believe the purpose of leadership is to develop your team in such a way that it can and will run itself."

Alan's eyebrows rise as if to say: "I don't believe you."

"Let me explain. When you lead any group, you will or you should mentor, teach, and coach them to grow and transform. To become better than they were before your leadership. They should be able to run the show in your absence. A leader's absence may be for a variety of reasons:

vacation, maternity leave, a sabbatical, or for a number of unplanned emergencies such as a medical or health crisis for either themselves or a loved one. Accidents happen and I've seen departments in a crisis because something happened to their leader. They weren't able to function because they weren't ready or prepared for the emergency or the absence of their leader."

Jack leans in, "Is your team ready today to handle your extended absence or an emergency?"

Alan slowly shakes his head no. He thinks to himself about the amount of guidance he gives to them daily, and how they rely on him for the big and small decisions. Their dependency on him is a daily frustration.

"I believe when a leader intentionally molds and teaches his team to work well with and without his presence, he'll have a team that clicks and knows what needs to get done in his absence. In other words, they don't need you to tell them what to do or to work at all. They become self-motivated and each member of the team motivates each other. They have a passion for what they do and they collectively do it really well. Each person understands why they're a part of the team. They step up to the plate, not because they have to but because they want to. They want to maintain or lift up the reputation of the department."

"How do I get them to that point?"

"There are a number of steps to getting there. I'm going to share with you what has worked for me in the past, with both great, talented teams and a group of people so disengaged that I was asked to take over and turn them around. But, I'm going to give this to you in pieces. Each piece I give you, must be added to what you already are doing. Each piece is part of a puzzle. And each piece matters."

"I can handle it; tell me what I need to know."

"No. I'm not going to do that because it would be too overwhelming for you and your team. I'll give it to you in segments or pieces. Over the coming months, we'll meet for lunch or at times I'll call you to give you the next piece of the puzzle. As you grow and change your leadership style skills, your team will shift with you. People like predictability, it makes us feel safe. If you change too much, they won't know who or what is happening. Small, gradual changes in the right direction will get you and your team moving in the right direction."

"I understand that. Why do you call it a puzzle?

"I refer to it as a puzzle because you need each piece to make the final masterpiece. Each piece is independent and connected to the others. But, like a puzzle, I am going to give you one piece at a time. Trust me, in the end, you will be happy and satisfied with the process and the final masterpiece. Everyone who is on your team may not know you are building a puzzle, but they will feel and experience the difference. I guarantee it!"

"Okay, a guarantee. I like that ... what do I get if it doesn't work?"

"Nothing," Jack chuckles. "It will work, if you're fully committed to the process I'm going to share with you."

"Got it, okay, tell me about the first piece of the puzzle."

"You are to start modeling the behavior you want your team to be doing, feeling, acting, and being like."

"That's it? Model behavior?"

"It's not as easy to model the behavior you want your team to have. First, you will have to decide on what that behavior is. What you are modeling. Refer back to the positive and negative leadership characteristics from our first lunch and your journaling."

"Can't you just tell me or share with me, which characteristics I should be modeling?"

"No," Jack pauses, "your style of leadership will be and should be different from mine or any other leader. There are similarities in great leadership. But that is the journey you are embarking on. I am not you, and therefore cannot tell you how to be the authentic leader you need to become. You will be a different but very effective leader. That I know about you."

Alan sighs a heavy exhale.

"You are developing new habits and that will accelerate your success. New habits start with making a choice and then taking action on that choice. The habits—or the type of leader you are today—are directly related to the habits you have today. Developing new habits takes discipline and to be consciously aware of them. In the beginning, during times of stress, we can revert back to our old comfortable but ineffective habits. Model the new habits you want for yourself and your team."

Silent, Alan takes in what his friend is sharing.

"I have to get going. I have a meeting to prepare for. Think about what I said; make the decision about whom you are becoming and start to model that. Make a list of the qualities or habits you will become as a leader. Then pick two and work on them today and over the next couple of weeks. Then add another to the mix."

Alan smiles, "Okay. Thanks for your time and I'll look forward to the next piece of the puzzle."

## Questions:

- What impact would you like your leadership to have on your team or company?

- Review the people you influence or lead, who needs personal or professional development?

- Create a development plan for each person in the previous question.

*Whoever is careless with the trust in small matters cannot be trusted with important matters.*

**-Albert Einstein**

# Chapter 4: Integrity and Trust

Coming from opposite ends of the street, Alan spots Jack walking towards the coffee shop. He waits at the door for his friend with a warm smile.

"Hey Jack," Alan greets his mentor, "How are you? How was the weekend?"

"Great, the weather was perfect for the wife and I to take a spontaneous trip up north. How about you?"

"My son had a little league game. He caught this fly ball and was so proud! I was a little proud of him too."

"That's great. So, how was your assignment-modeling the behaviors you want to see in your team?"

"Not as easy as I thought it was going to be. I essentially forgot, as soon as I got back to the fires on my desk. You were right; we resort back to old or comfortable ways when stress is part of the equation. I had to set reminders on my cell phone and a few discreet sticky notes on my desk. I started by modeling listening skills and asking better questions."

"What did you notice, in yourself or your team?"

"Well, and I'll be honest here, it was hard. But I noticed how much more information I learned when I took the time to really hear what they were saying, when I gave them the space to talk and share. At first, I wanted to interrupt with my thoughts or suggestions, but I stopped myself and really listened. I also noticed by being consistent with this new habit, they started sharing more and asking more questions of me. My biggest surprise was I saw their energy levels rising with mine and amongst each other. It was as if no one had ever listened to them before."

"Sounds like it made you feel good, like you got more out of doing less, or in the case of listening, doing something different."

"Yes, and I don't know if they did this consciously, but I noticed them listening to each other. I didn't only practice this at the office. I took it home with me. I knew what I was doing. My wife and kids kind of looked at me funny listening to them as they spoke."

"Great, let's add on to that. Today's puzzle piece is integrity. How would you define integrity?"

Alan takes a deep breath, "Well, if we don't have integrity, we don't really have anything. It's our word. It's who we are. It's holding true to ourselves and our core beliefs. Walking your talk."

Jack interjects, "Yes, 'walking your talk,' and how often are you not walking your talk?"

"Oh," Alan starts to get a little defensive, "Well, I think that ... you know ... I'm true to my word all the time."

Jack tilts his head and smirks a bit, "Do you follow through with the answers to questions for your team, when you say you will? Are you getting home on time when you tell your wife that you'll be home for dinner? Are you showing up at your kid's games, when you say you'll be there? Or are you making excuses?"

"I thought that we were talking about work."

"It all blends together. Leadership is not something you do during office hours, and then place it neatly in your desk drawer and come back to on the following business day. It's who you are, it's who you are becoming."

"That was in the book you sent over. Well, in that case, there are times I tell my wife I'll be home, and I'm probably an hour late. But she's understanding. And, there are times when I'm not able to be at the kids' games. When I see them later, I tell them *Daddy had to work late, something came up*, and they understand."

"Yes, they will understand. Here's what I know, if you're not holding true to your word in one area of your life, there's another area of your life, or more where you're not holding true to your word. It can be something as simple as the meeting starts at 10 a.m. and you don't show up until 10:05 or 10:10 because you're preparing or running behind. That sets a precedent; you're not true to your word. People start to learn that about you. They respond in accordance to your behavior; they show up late to the meeting because they know you won't be there on time, so why should they? Leadership sets the tone."

Alan is speechless.

"Alan, I know the truth is hard to hear. Someone had the courage to share this with me. You've got to be the person your team can trust and depend on. Your wife and kids for that matter too. They need to trust your word, and if you say you're going to start the meeting at 10:00, then you start that meeting at 10:00 and not 10:07. If you say that you're going to have a one-on-one meeting with one of your associates or get an answer to a question-you make it happen. Whenever you say you're going to do something, you do it. A hurricane or blizzard should be the only thing preventing you, but with the technology, there's always a way. You know what I mean."

They both chuckle.

"Your team needs to know, along with your family, you are committed to them. Leadership is not just what you do, it's who you become.

"Let's talk about trust, which goes hand in hand with integrity and commitment. They seem to be the three words that are the theme of today's puzzle piece. I remember you telling me you weren't sure of the level of trust you had for your team. There's a way to improve that.

"Trust is earned. It's not a given. People learn to trust you through your words, but more importantly from your actions. I remember my parents saying 'actions speak louder than words.' For people to follow you, when you're developing a high-performing team, trust is part of the foundation. From trust comes commitment. Trust also comes from honesty. When you're honest with your team, honest about your thoughts, your feelings, feedback, not making excuses, your relationships will change. Integrity, trust, and commitment are the foundation to great leadership. The stronger that foundation, the more impact your leadership will have.

"I want you to stand tall and be the honorable person who is developing a high-performance team, but who's also an outstanding citizen outside of the office and a wonderful family man. This is something that you do 24/7. I remember Stephen Covey once saying, you should act in a way as if you were walking in freshly fallen snow, when look back you can see exactly where you've been. And so can everyone else. That to me is integrity when people know what you represent, they trust who you are and know that you are true to your word. It's not always easy in the business world because there are lots of people who think of integrity as 'is it convenient for me?' I learned a long time ago, doing the right thing is not always the easiest thing to do but it will carry you through life."

"Thanks, Jack. You've given me a lot to think about. I'm not making any excuses. I'm taking full responsibility for this foundation. I know what I try to do, but maybe I'm not always in alignment with as much integrity that I thought I was or want to be."

"Great. This is what I want you to work on this month. This is an important lesson. This lays down the foundation for who you are and who you are becoming. Think about this. Every day, reflect back on the day, where you might have slipped little in these these areas. Awareness is half the battle. The more aware you are, the easier things will move forward. Reflection is a part of raising your bar. Acknowledge your slip ups and do better next time."

## Questions:

- How is integrity important to you and what you do?

- What times or events are you more likely to modify integrity?

- What would you like your new personal rule on trust and integrity to be?

*You can have everything in life you want, if you will just help others get what they want.*

**-Zig Ziglar**

# Chapter 5: A Subtle Piece

Glancing out at the skyline of the city, Alan sips his morning cup of coffee before the team arrives at the office. He reflects on the past month since his last meeting with Jack.

     His team is coming together and he's seeing more initiative in his people stepping up and taking more responsibility. *Being true to my word and honoring my promises is building trust and stronger bonds with others.* His stress level has decreased a few notches, because his team is working like a team and he trusts them more, and they trust him more. Understanding, more than ever, this really is a lifelong journey and not something you learn in a weekend seminar. You can't possibly become a great leader after eight hours in a classroom. *No, this really is a lifelong journey. As much as I was impatient and wanted all the information to be a great leader, in the beginning; I appreciate the time this is taking, to really step into my true leader. To become the best version of myself, will reflect in my leadership style.*

The phone rings. Alan spins around and picks it up on the second ring, "Hey, Jack, morning."

"Hey, how are you doing this morning?"

"Great. I've been getting to the office a little early on most days to prepare for the day, before the hustle and bustle starts. I'm able to look at the day and even the days ahead to prepare and plan them out, setting my goals and deciding on what my desired outcome is for each meeting. Quite frankly, I'm finding myself to be a little less stressed and more in control."

"That's great to hear and I'm sure your team is feeling it too," Jack says. "Well, let's get down to it, as I only have a short window. I'm sure you've got a cup of coffee and I've got mine. Today, I want to talk to you about the awareness of others, really being in tune with others. You've heard of emotional intelligence?"

Alan shakes his head, "I've heard about it, but haven't read much on the topic, to be honest."

"It's been around for quite a while, and emotional intelligence is really what separates fair leaders from outstanding leaders. The more you understand people and what drives them, the more you will understand why they do what they do. So the awareness of others is just one part of emotional intelligence. I want you to really listen and feel what other people are feeling. Notice what people say and what they don't say. Listen to their choice of words, how and when they pause, for example. There is meaning in pauses. Notice how they move or stand; watch their body language. I want you to really feel the emotions coming from others, the energy or the tension that's in a room. The energy or tension that's between two people having a conversation.

"Be a private investigator or a research scientist. I want you to observe people and start to study their behaviors, what they say, their movements. Become in tune with others that you could close your eyes and hear their emotions. I want it so that if you were playing your day as a silent movie, you would be able to understand, without any words, what's really going on. Being able to pick out those emotions and what's happening comes with this awareness level. Study and look at your own reaction to things, the choice of words you use. Awareness is so important to figuring it out. It's such an integral part of leadership."

"Wow," Alan says, "this sounds like something that I'll be able to do everywhere. So should I be practicing and honing the skill not just at the office, but maybe at social events, kids' games or during my commute to work?"

"Oh yes, everywhere. Just be an observer of people and study them. You're going to learn so much, and it will help you in your reactions and responses."

"Fantastic, I'm up to the challenge."

"Well, great, have a great week. Check in via e-mail and let me know how you're doing. I'll be traveling this week."

"Again, Jack, thank you for this and everything else that you've done for me. I look forward to this."

"You're welcome. You're doing a great job. Bye."

Hanging up the phone, Alan takes a deep breath. "No better time than the present to try this," he thinks. His next meeting isn't for another hour. Rising from his desk, he decides to take a walk around his department.

As he passes Mary's desk, they make eye contact. She doesn't say a word. Following him with her narrowing eyes, keeping her head fixed and never missing a beat as she types away at her keyboard. "Click, click, click," is all Alan hears as he walks away.

Turning the corner out of his office, he sees Karen and Doug having a discussion and pointing to the tablet they're working on. They make eye contact with Alan but quickly look back down, hoping to go unnoticed.

"Morning, what are you two engrossed with?" Alan questions with a smile.

Both of them hesitate for a moment and finally Karen speaks up, "Um, we're going over the new client's numbers for the past six months for their proposal."

Doug adds, "We're trying to do some of the leg work now to discuss at our next department meeting on Monday."

Alan senses they are uncomfortable because it is unusual for him to be out of his office unless there's a problem. Wanting them to feel more at ease and more trusting of him, he quickly thinks about what to do.

Wanting to show respect to them, he asks, "Mind if I sit down with you?"

"Okay," Karen and Doug say in unison.

Grabbing a chair from an unoccupied desk to come across casually, Alan sits backwards in the chair with his arms crossed on the back. "What ya got?"

Again, they are stumbling for words and Alan can sense he needs to make them comfortable. Quickly.

"You both have great ideas and solutions for our clients and I'd love to hear your thoughts so far."

Hearing that, Karen begins to smile as Doug exhales. They both take turns sharing what they are seeing and the different ideas they have for the proposal. The conversation quickly turns into a brainstorming session of ideas to share at the next department meeting.

Alan excuses himself to get to his next appointment. Pleased with his progress, and feeling proud of himself and his team.

## Questions:

- How can you apply the lessons in this chapter to your daily life?

- What benefit would this have to your leadership style?

- What benefits would it have on the people you're leading and influencing?

*Frustration is a sign I am acting independently. The more you try your own way, the tighter the doors will stay closed.*

**-Joyce Meyer**

# Chapter 6: Misunderstanding and Frustration

Mary has her routine and you don't dare try and change that. Every afternoon around 2:00 p.m., she's missing from her desk. That's when she takes a walk to get some fresh air and some java to keep her motors running for the remainder of the day. Not every day, but most. Some days, she takes that walk to keep her job, otherwise she might snap at some unknowing person as they casually walk by her desk. But those are on the few, bad, hectic stressful days. Most days she's successful at managing her emotions and having her positive can-do attitude.

It must be mid afternoon. There's Mary sitting at her desk, typing up several new memos regarding procedure changes, with a Venti something or other within arms' reach. Soft music is coming from her cell phone as she types and sways to the beat. Life is good.

Alan storms right by her without even a hello. Smirking, she knows this means trouble when he doesn't ask about messages. Leaning back in her chair, she peeks through the open door to determine his mood. She can see him sitting at his desk, leaning back and looking at the ceiling with that frustrated look she has seen too many times. Taking one more big, long sip and whispering, "Ahhhh, that's what I need before entering the Lion's Den."

"What?" she says, leaning in the doorway.

"What nothing."

"Mmmm, you know I know something happened. So spill it." Giving Alan time to gather his thoughts, she takes it upon herself to sit in the chair across from the desk. "You know, I think I want one of these chairs, instead of the one at my desk. This is much more comfortable for me."

"Huh?"

"I'd get more work done."

"I doubt it."

"Do you have a complaint?"

"No, you're great."

"Thank you. Spill it, what happened to you on your way up here?"

"Nothing."

"Go on. You know, I'm not leaving this very comfortable chair until you start talking," as she rubs the arms of the fine grade leather.

"Promise? It's ... just that sometimes," choosing his words carefully.

"Stop it, it's me and I'm here to help. Do you need a Venti something with whipped cream on the top?"

Alan finally smiles and chuckles. "No, but thanks for the offer. Sometimes, I feel like I'm talking to a stone wall. I give them instructions, share the goal with them and they just stare at me. Like they don't get it at all."

"When you say 'them,' I'm presuming you're talking about them?" she points out the door referring to the team.

He nods. "I don't feel like we're on the same page. I'm trying to be the engaging leader to get these piles of emergencies done and taken care of."

Mary slowly starts shaking her head, "You just don't get it."

"What don't I get?"

"I've been wait'n for you to finally say something."

Alan looks puzzled and leans in, elbows on his desk.

"You don't understand them. I've noticed you and the team don't get each other," she says with emphasis on the words each other.

"No."

"You've never worked with this kind of group."

"No. What is the problem with them?"

"It ain't them, it's you."

"What?"

"There is a huge generational gap between you and them. You don't understand them and they don't understand you. The only way to bridge this gap is for you to make that gap much smaller. You need to understand them; they are the future generation that will be leading this company one day and our country for that matter."

"Okay, what do I do? I need one more thing to do, like I need a hole in the head."

"Oh, poor you. Trust me, when you figure this one out, it will make being a great leader much easier, much, much easier."

He looks up at Mary, feeling doubtful.

"I know someone that will help you."

"Great give me their number and I'll call them right now."

"Call?" The look on Mary's face reads disbelief.

"E-mail?"

"E-mail? You need more help than I thought." Shaking her head again and laughing, she pivots to leave the room. As she's walking out she shouts, "Text. You text."

"Text?" he mutters under his breath. The only time he texts is when he doesn't want to tell his wife he's late leaving the office and doesn't want to hear her comments. Of course that doesn't stop her when he gets home. She has embraced the technology more so than he, who still believes in face to face or phone conversations. *I guess that's just one example of how I need to manage this gap.*

## Questions:

- Where do you find yourself frustrated or wasting energy?

- How many different generations do you mange or interact with? Which ones?

- How is your interaction different with the various generations?

*Have patience. All things are difficult*
*before they become easy.*

**-Saadi**

# Chapter 7: An Unlikely Mentor

Entering the cafe, Alan thinks about how he had passed by this place many times not giving it a second thought. "I don't even know who I'm looking for," he mutters as he scans around the place. It is lunchtime and the place is busy with all the tables filled with food, or some type of electronic device. He remembers Mary's words, "She'll find you, and keep an open mind."

He stands there looking around, feeling more uncomfortable with each passing second. Not sure what to do, he heads for the counter to order a sandwich and kill some time, maybe return to the office if she doesn't show.

"Alan," a pleasant voice comes from behind him as she approaches him.

"Hi, I'm Ava," she says, extending a hand.

"Nice to meet you. I'm ordering a sandwich, can I get you one?"

"I'm good, my table is right over there."

Sitting down, removing his jacket, he notices he's the only person wearing a jacket and tie and suddenly he feels a little out of place. But he's willing to be uncomfortable in his environment to learn.

This young woman has flawless, cocoa-colored skin, and hair braided and piled high on top of her head. She has as many earrings to match the numerous bracelets hanging from her petite wrist. She looks more like a college student, and he wonders what he could actually learn from this meeting that he didn't already know.

"Mary speaks very highly of you. How do you two know each other?"

"She's my favorite aunt," she tells him, smiling.

"Tell me about yourself, since Mary didn't tell me about you at all."

"In a nutshell, I'm on a philanthropic team for a hospital not too far from here, just outside of the city. I went to school for the arts and I'm the lead singer for a band. We do mostly local venues. It's fun."

"So you ask people for money?"

"No, actually, the team does that. I guide the team and strategize the big picture for all of us to work towards. We all work together on a number of projects, but I've been there the longest and know most of our regular donors very, very well."

Alan is a bit surprised that she is running a department at a hospital, let alone running any kind of department. She seems too young to have that level of responsibility, not to mention her choice in wardrobe today. She isn't dressed like someone who would talk to donors, in her leggings, flats, and oversized sweater. Nothing about her says "corporate"; you would easily assume she worked as a barista, or maybe a kindergarten teacher.

"Aunt Mary said you were having problems relating to your team members. She asked me to share with you what our generation needs and wants in the workplace, to not just survive, but really grow and become an asset."

"Yes, and thank you for taking the time to share with me. I don't know if I would say I can't relate to them. I feel they're unmotivated. How do I motive and inspire this group of people? I'm in a leadership role that brings a great deal of responsibility."

"I'm gonna be real honest with you, if that's okay, and some of it might sting a little bit. You okay with that?"

Alan nodded and she continues. "First, let's approach leadership from a different perspective: mentoring. They are not unmotivated; you haven't figured out how to unlock their potential. No offense, but my aunt says you're real good at barking out orders."

"I don't bark out orders, I highly suggest a certain approach to the problems and guide them to the right solutions."

"Right, that sounds like barking, yelling, telling them what to do instead of working together. We, and I'm speaking for them, are smart, creative problem solvers, when given the chance. You might find out how creative and innovative your team is at solving problems even before problems arise. But you have to give them a chance to think, to prove themselves, and use their skills. It might not be your way. As a matter of fact, I bet it will be a different approach than any one you've thought of.

"Your department cannot be great because of only you. You have a great department or team of people because you invest and develop them. That's what they—or we—want: to be invested in, to learn and develop."

"O-ka-y," he says, dragging out the syllables. "I've heard that before."

"I'll move on, since we're short on time, although I wish more people would be open to our new way of working and living. Which brings me to my second point. We were born with the Internet, computers, tablets and smartphones. We don't know a world without it. The generations before us got introduced to this connected world. The Internet is a great tool. It's has made us very resourceful, and the social media component has created engagement; not only locally, but globally. We are accustomed to knowing what is going on in our friends' lives, even the ones we haven't seen or spoken to for quite a while. Social media has lifted the veil, and transparency is for all to see. Look around the Internet and you'll see what people are confessing, showing us how to do or what they're doing, and I'll admit not all of it we need to be sharing. I mean some stuff should stay behind closed doors, but oh well."

"So, I bet your wondering how this translates to the workplace, which is what you really want to know. Two words: engagement and transparency. Be honest and open with all that you can be open and honest about. They, we, want to be a part of the information cycle. Share with us what's going on in the organization, above, below and laterally. When you are open and transparent we feel like we're respected, valued, and a part of the team, the organization.

"A side note to that is also feedback. Yearly reviews are great, and they're really so someone can check a box and say it was completed. But why should I only hear about what I'm doing well and what areas need improvements only once a year? You wouldn't hesitate to pull someone aside and have a talk, if they were screwing up, right?"

Alan nods.

"Then why not take every opportunity to give positive feedback when you see it? Encourage good ideas and foresee potential problems. Be free with your comments of gratitude. Ask questions instead of giving away the answer. Get to know us, personally, and be open or transparent about yourself."

Alan is all ears as he finishes the last bites of his sandwich. "What am I suppose to be transparent about?"

"What do you talk about with your friends?"

"Stuff: the game, my wife and kids ... umm, work stuff, I guess."

"When you share things with us, things either in or out of the office, I feel you trust me. That trust goes a long way because I learn I can trust you. If I know who you are, and not just some bossy guy in the corner office, I feel connected to you and the team as whole."

Alan stares at her; it was all starting to make sense, slowly.

She continues, "Once upon a time, people went to work for a paycheck. Their work didn't need to have or give them purpose. Go to work, earn a paycheck, come home and support your family. Back then, most people got their fulfillment from other places outside of work: their neighborhood, church, civic groups, etc. Today, people want —and I think need—to feel their work is purposeful and fulfills them emotionally, not only financially. Create an environment in your department, with your team, that feeds that fulfillment part of us.

"Which brings me to the third: Purpose. We want to know, the work that we're doing is for a greater good. We aren't just working to make the guy at the top able to buy another yacht or get a bigger bonus each year. Does my work improve the world around me? Help someone? Are we creating something profound? We need to feel that connection to our work via the purpose."

"I'm starting to see a connection, pun intended. This generation wants to feel connected to others and their work. They grew up with the Internet that connected them globally to people and information. As the person in the leadership position, I need to create an environment of connection by engaging with them from their perspective. Essentially, helping them meet their needs, which will help me and the company meet its needs.

"Now, the part about connecting their fulfillment with the purpose of our work sounds odd but I can understand why. I need to help them feel connected to the company's purpose, why we do what we do. If I can help them see the bigger picture, share the story about what we do and who it helps, they'll see it."

"And if they can see it, they'll feel it too," she says, excited for him. "What do you think that will do for performance?"

Alan runs his fingers through his hair while leaning way back in his chair. "Alive."

"What?"

"When 'they,' or let's take your generation, for example; when you feel more connected you're more alive. The more alive you feel, the more in the game you'll be. You'll play at your A game, sharing and using all of your skills and talents. It's my responsibility to create this connection between each of them and what we do and who we are as a group."

She shakes her head in agreement and smiles.

"I bet this new way of leadership would also help with turnover rates and filling open positions."

"Yes, you'll be able to maintain a higher level of talent, creating this kind of team and department culture to work in."

"I recently read an article about this."

"Good, then it's not the first time you've heard about this stuff."

"No. This has been enlightening. I found your explanations of why they want these things to make sense. I understand much better."

"Great, if you have any question, feel free to text me. I have to run now."

"Yes, okay. Thank you, I will," and she is off, headed out and on her way to her next meeting, he guesses.

## Questions:

- What surprises you about younger generations from yourself to work with?

- What benefits do you see other generations contributing to the work place?

- What can you learn from other generations?

*Tell me and I forget. Teach me and I remember. Involve me and I learn.*

**-Benjamin Franklin**

# Chapter 8: Managing Ourselves

Alan swings open the door to the usual meeting place. The lunch crowd has returned to their offices, allowing for a quieter atmosphere for conversations. The hostess, standing behind the desk, smiles to greet him and points to the window across the room. He sees Jack relaxing at one of the tables.

"Alan, I see you are really practicing being on time. I had a meeting, nearby, that finished up earlier than expected."

"Well, thank you. This is one of my new habits. I don't know anything else but to be ten to fifteen minutes early. Everywhere and every day."

The waitress approaches with a pitcher of water and shares the daily specials. They both get lost in conversation about their families, a new client of Jack's, and the renovation project Alan and his wife are tackling.

When lunch is served, Jack starts the conversation, "Let's talk about your leadership journey. How's everything? What did you learn when you increased your awareness of others?"

Alan lets out a long sigh before he starts, "I cannot believe all of the information that I've been missing, when I'm not aware of others. What people say and what they don't say and their emotions ... it's a wealth of information to be able to pick up on something and know that it's either out of character for them or that there is something more, that they're giving an answer that they think I or the rest of the group wants to hear. I got really curious about it and was able to draw it out a little more with questions. I noticed how much more information they shared with me, and that's how I was able to, like at work, uncover some of the problems that were going on and be able to nip them in the bud before they became really big problems."

"What else did you notice?"

A familiar "bing!" sings from Alan's phone.

"At the end of the day, on my commute home, I reflected on previous conversations I had. During this reflection time, I realized what other information I missed or what question I should have asked. I'm learning from those moments as well. Sorry about this, I thought it was on silent."

"No problem. Do you need to check it?"

"Yes. I'm embracing texting because it's how my team want to communicate with me and each other." Alan reads the message and smiles a bit.

"Looks like a nice message, yes?" Jack inquires, practicing his awareness skills.

"My team is letting me know they finished the big proposal we've all been working really hard on. Let me respond to them." Alan smiles as a proud leader and hits send.

"I like this version of Alan."

"Thanks, I'm really liking this version too. You were saying?"

"What changes have you seen in your team?"

Alan pauses for a moment, while he pours cream into his coffee and slowly stirs, staring at the cup. Looking up at Jack, he finally says, "Hmm, I noticed a slight comfort that comes with being understood. I believe, since I'm picking up on this missed information, I'm more in tune with them and where they are. As a result, I ask different questions. It's a little difficult to put into words."

"Sounds like your being fully present and employee engagement is rising. Keep working on this, and never stop doing it. This ties in nicely with today's topic: managing yourself."

Alan wants to cut his friend off and he quickly realizes it is because he wants to defend himself. He always manages himself well. Jack has great advice and is one of the best mentors he could have. He's so grateful for these lunches and the lessons to help him become not only a good leader, but the type of leader that others want to follow, not one they have to follow. He focuses again on Jack's words.

"As a leader, it's not only our job, but our responsibility to keep those we lead safe. Feeling safe is a basic human need. When people feel safe, they work and act in a place where fear does not and cannot exist. Fear, neurologically, can cripple us. Our brains are designed to keep us safe and out of danger. There is a part of the brain that detects and responds to danger very quickly.

"For example, you're driving down the highway and suddenly you see brake lights. Our subconscious brain responds to this danger by instructing your foot to hit the brakes. You stay safe, you didn't rear-end the car in front of you and you don't give it much thought. It would take too long for our subconscious brain to tell the conscious brain, 'Hey brake lights, what should I do here? Is there immediate —' Slam! you've hit the car front of you.

"Our subconscious brains are designed to detect danger. When it does, we go into that fight mode. Our people are the same; they can pick up clues from you that you may not be aware of. As their leader, similar to parenting, we keep our team or family safe."

Alan looks a little confused, "Would you apply this to my work life? I want to be sure I really understand what you're sharing with me."

"Yes. For example, let's say you come out of a stressful meeting with your superiors. A major project has been terminated because of faulty data; the customer changed their mind and went in a different direction; or there were mechanical defects. You are personally stressed, frustrated, and upset by the loss of this project because of the man-hours you and your team have put in. Now you walk into a staff meeting to discuss budget plans for the following year, or you're interviewing a new candidate. I want you to choose the right emotions versus reacting. When we react, we lose control. When you lose control, you make bad choices and become victim to what I call unproductive emotions.

"You can get better results from your team if they know you handle stressful situations in a manner that is professional and not threatening to them."

Alan thinks about this briefly, "Like you. I remember on numerous occasions, we, as a team, had bad news to share with you about a customer, project or a big account. I never felt anxious or uncomfortable about delivering bad news to you because you took it in a predictable manner. You were helpful and never upset. You might have been disappointed with the disclosure, like we were but never mad at us. Thinking about it now, I would have to say you were part of the solution, and never dumped it back on us. Because of the way you handled the negative report we were able to offer our ideas and solutions."

"Thank you. That's what I want you to work on next: controlling any bad or unproductive emotions. Be part of the solution and welcome uncomfortable conversation along with the good news. I know you won't slip up on this learning tip, but if you do, apologize for being unprofessional and disrespectful. An apology goes a long way and you will be forgiven. But you're not going to slip up," Jack says, with a sarcastic tone.

They both laugh as they stand up to head out the door together.

Alan's afternoon meeting is fairly easy and uneventful. He looks out over the city from his office window reflecting on his session with Jack and the encounters he had with his team that afternoon. His mood was greatly affected by whatever problem was front and center. He would go from meeting to meeting infecting his negative mood on others. He got the results, which earned him his promotions, but at what costs? There were many nights his wife would tell the kids to leave Daddy alone; he had a bad day at work. That was going to come to an end, immediately.

He glances at his watch; it is time to leave. He sent his wife a text message earlier that afternoon, stating they would be going out to dinner as a family. He's sure she'll be very skeptical and has a backup plan if he's not home on time. He grabs his jacket and heads for the door; she was not going to execute that plan B tonight.

Glancing at his laptop, he decides to leave it. Tonight, he is only going to be a dad and a husband.

## Questions:

- How have people misinterpreted your emotions in the past?

- As someone who is leading and making an impact, how should you mange your emotions?

- What benefits would you experience with better emotion management?

*Without a struggle, there can be no progress.*

*-Frederick Douglass*

# Chapter 9: The E-mail

The Monday morning weekly planning meeting with the team is underway. Alan takes every opportunity to apply the lessons he is learning. He's asking more questions and listening to what the team says and their ideas. When Alan does ask a question or makes a comment, he gives the space or time for them to think before they voice their opinions.

"What else could we do?" has become one of Alan's common questions to generate conversation. These days his team does more of the talking and running the meetings. This is a significant change from when he began in this position, when he would run the meetings.

"Well, everyone, I think this was a very successful meeting today. Everyone understands what their responsibilities are for this week. Is there anything I missed, Alan?" Karen asks. It is her turn to run this week's meetings.

Alan shakes his head, "I'm happy with our progress today."

Everyone gathers their items and retreats from the conference room. Alan has made it a point to get the team to do more of the talking and sharing during the meetings. It has happened slowly with some trepidation. Alan asks and listens more. With some patience and time the team feels more at ease about sharing openly.

More recently, he shared with them some of the basics to running a meeting. They are allowed to give their input on how they want to structure their meetings: length of time, frequency, holding each other accountable, and being prepared, for example. Alan then introduced the idea that each team member rotate into the role of running the meeting. Everyone would gain valuable experience, and if Alan was not able to attend the meetings they would still be held in his absence.

Karen is wiping down the white board.

"Karen, you did a great job."

"Thank you, I was a bit nervous."

"You couldn't tell at all."

Karen stands a little taller and smiles brighter, pleased with this acknowledgement.

Noticing how she is trying to hide her pride, Alan decides to give her more feedback. "I know this was only your second time running these project meetings, but you handled the tangent very well getting the team back on task. And you got everything done in a very timely manner. As a matter of fact you finished twelve minutes early," he tells her, looking at his watch.

"Thank you for noticing. I tried and I didn't feel the need to take up the whole hour, since there's a ton of work to get done before the next meeting, which I'm running by the way."

"Really?"

"Yes, Chris has a personal matter and asked if I could fill in."

"That was very generous of you. How's everything else going for you?"

Pausing only briefly and looking away from Alan's gaze, "Ahh, good."

Picking up on Karen's tone and breaking the eye contact, Alan senses there is something going on. "Hmm, just good? Sounds like there's something. Please share, if you feel comfortable, you are a valuable member of this team and I'm here to help."

"Okay, there's a class over at the university that I'm taking to finish up my master's degree. It's two days a week but I've been late to the class since it started."

"I didn't know you were in school. How many more classes till you finish?"

"Four, including this one."

"Okay, how can I help?"

"Well, I was thinking, would it be okay if I changed my hours? I could come in earlier, to make up the time, or work longer on other days, to get my part of the project done, or …"

"I'm glad you are continuing to learn and I admire your dedication. Do whatever you need to do to get to class on time, get your work here done, and have enough energy to study. I trust you and your fellow team members trust you too. Be open with them, like you've been here with me."

"Really? Thank you. This is huge," the tone in her voice reaching higher with excitement. "I really appreciate it."

"Good. Thanks for being part of my team."

"Okay, I gotta go. I have things to get done, so I can leave a bit early today. Thank you, you won't be disappointed."

Alan smiles with satisfaction as he watches her rush out of the room, knowing this little gift to her would pay off in the short and long term.

The old version of him would have rushed out of the room after the meeting to return to his office and retrieve messages. He would have lost the opportunity to give positive feedback and see how she shined hearing the positive words. He also would have missed the opportunity to learn something new about her and a dream that she was pursuing.

How many opportunities had he missed in the past? Too many, but he vows to be the best leader he can be for his team, and he will not miss those opportunities to impact others.

Approaching Mary's desk, she looks up, "What are you smiling about?"

"I'm not smiling."

"Oh yes you are, you look like the Cheshire Cat. What d'ya do now?"

"Nothing. I had a nice moment with Karen, if you must know."

"She do a good job running the meeting—doing your job?"

"Excellent. It's not my job to run all the meetings. I want them to be comfortable running meetings here because it will prepare them for the future."

"I know what you're doing. But why are you smiling, cuz it's more than just that."

"I asked how she was doing and I could tell there was something. She asked for some flexibility in her hours so she could leave early a few days a week."

"For her master's. That was nice of you."

"How did you know?"

"I know things. You gotta talk to them and make it a habit of getting to know them."

"I'm trying."

"I know you are, and don't think they don't see the changes in you also."

"But how did you know?"

"I just do, because I know everything going on in this office." She spun on her chair away from Alan and back to her keyboard with a smirk across her face.

"You most certainly do," he mutters.

The next morning, Alan glances over the skyline from his office. Getting to work early not only gives him enough time to prepare for the day, it gives him a sense of peace and confidence. He's taken control of his morning, instead of letting others control his day. Thinking about the awareness of others, he opens up his laptop to write an e-mail.

Jack,

I trust your business travels are going well this week. I wanted to touch base with you regarding my assignment, being aware of others.

Because I'm sensing more with my team, I ask questions instead of brushing it off. People are willing to share when they are asked. I'm noticing how the relationships with each of my team members are strengthening.

The other night, when I returned home in time for dinner with the family, I used these skills. I noticed my wife's energy level was different. Her smile was forced and she was focused on the vegetables she was cutting. I could actually feel the tension, which I never noticed before or brushed away.

I decided to give her a hug from behind and asked her what was on her mind. At first she said nothing and I didn't believe her so I asked again. Eventually, she turned around and told me she was feeling alone and tired of everything. I listened and focused on her as she spoke and didn't get defensive. She needed to be heard and feel loved.

It's amazing, what listening and focusing on another does for the overall relationship. I've made it a goal to give my team the attention they need to succeed at every opportunity available to me and my wife gets my undivided attention when I walk in the door.


Thank you,

Alan


The next morning an e-mail arrives from Jack.


Hello Alan,

I'm pleased you're using these skills not just in the office but at home. The skills I'm sharing with you are the foundation to great leadership. Great leadership is based on solid relationships-both personal and professional.

Tell your lovely wife I said hello.


Regards,

Jack

## Questions:

- Make a list of your personal and professional accomplishments. Which ones are your biggest assets?

- How have you grown as a leader?

- Where have you grown or stretched your abilities lately?

*One way to boost our will power and focus is to manage our distractions instead of letting them manage us.*
**-Daniel Coleman**

# Chapter 10: Focusing

"We live in a very distracting world. We have e-mails, text messages, TVs, phones ringing, people demanding our attention. The list goes on, and there are so many things that our minds can become so easily distracted by. People are multitasking, if not, triple-tasking. That's a new word, I just made it up. Research has proven that there is no such thing as effective multitasking. If you multitask, your actions are equivalent to a drunken hamster, running around in circles and not getting anywhere quickly. Concentrate on one thing. That's how our brains are designed; that's how they function at their best. While you're developing your high-performance teams and role modeling outstanding leadership skills, one of them should be focus, to concentrate and put your focus on whatever it is that you're doing at the time and not several things at once."

Alan

"That's going to be really difficult. I know that I multitask. As a matter of fact, I might be addicted to it." Grabbing for a bottled water to hand to his mentor, while catching his breath sitting on the bench, he realizes Jack is in great shape for his age. Alan definitely needs to make getting in shape a priority.

"Thanks. At least you're aware of your addiction. Remember what I use to say?"

"Yes, awareness is half the battle. How often do you run?"

"Weekends only, during the week I hit the gym."

Still catching his breath Alan comments, "Man, you're in great shape."

"Thanks. Running helps me stay focused. Any new habit is uncomfortable at first. Do it for a week or two and then at the end of that time, if you don't like the results, you can go back to your old unproductive ways."

"Yeah, I've heard that one before. I think from years ago when I used to work for you," he says sarcastically.

Jack smiles and chuckles, "So when you're working on a presentation, shut down your e-mail. Figure out when your best and most productive times are. You need to go through your schedule and figure out, 'Here's when I'm planning to work on this task or project.' If it's not scheduled, it doesn't get done, and that way when you're working on a particular project, you shut off the e-mail on your computer. Shut off or put your phone in airplane mode or put it on silent. I don't even want you to see it going off because it will just distract you and you'll want to know *Who is that text message from? Who's that e-mail from? Who's calling?* Completely focus on the tasks at hand."

"But, I get more done when I multitask. Or I feel like I do."

"Feel like you do. But when you focus on doing one thing at a time, you actually become more efficient. You will get tasks done in a shorter amount of time."

"But—"

"But nothing. This is not an easy one. You will have to break the multitasking habit. But what I have found, it not only helped me be more productive, it impacted my energy level and relationships."

"Relationships?"

Jack smiles, "Yes, relationships. How many times are you in a conversation with someone and thinking about what you need to do next, an e-mail you need to compose, a repair on the house?"

"Okay, doesn't everyone do that?"

"No. I want you to be fully present when you're with someone to build that relationship and you'll get more done. Doesn't this remind you a little bit of another lesson?"

"Yes, the awareness of others and building trust. Letting others know they're valued and I respect them and their time will build stronger bonds."

Jack smiles and says, "Yes, grasshopper."

•

# Questions:

- Is multitasking one of your habits? How could you modify this behavior?

- How will your relationships benefit with more focused attention?

- What benefits would focusing add to your productivity?

*It's the passionate person that influences others and changes the world. What are you passionate about? What are you changing?*
**-Laurie-Ann Murabito**

# Chapter 11: The Final Lesson

Alan pulls open the door to their meeting place. This is a new location, which he's heard great reviews for. He approaches the hostess, who greets him warmly.

"I'm meeting a friend here for lunch and I'm not sure if—"

She interrupts with, "Mr. Robbins is expecting you. Please follow me."

Alan follows her; the tables are all busy with lunchtime meetings and social gatherings. You can tell by the diners' attire and the expressions on their faces: casual and gleeful, or jackets and serious.

"Here you go, sir, enjoy your lunch."

Jack extends his hand, "Alan, how are you?"

"I'm good," he says as he seats himself across the table for two. "I've been wanting to try this place for some time now. I hear great things and the reviews. Thanks for suggesting it."

"It is one of my favorite restaurants. I do come here often with clients and my wife. They know me well here and I've had the pleasure of meeting the head chef. We'll try the cheese steak egg rolls. You won't be disappointed."

"Well, now I'm really looking forward to lunch, and possibly a future date night with my wife."

As their plates are being cleared, Alan leans back in his chair, wondering what today's lesson will be. He's come so far because of Jack. He can see the change in his team and others notice too. In between these meetings, he had to do the work, learn new habits, develop his awareness of others, and take in constructive feedback. All along this journey he has noticed how more self-aware he has become. *Becoming open about one's own self learning is the biggest gift any of us could have. Maybe, that's the greatest puzzle piece.*

Stopping by with a silver coffee carafe, the waiter fills their porcelain cups. The aroma of freshly brewed coffee permeates the air. As Alan stirs in cream, he looks up at Jack and asks, "What do I get to work on this month?"

"I like how you word that, 'I get to work on.' That speaks of gratitude."

"Yes, I am grateful for all you've done and how these meetings have changed me and changed my team. I actually catch my team smiling when they're in the office, and not only when they're leaving for the day."

Jack smiles as he nods. "Alan, today, I want to share with you what every outstanding leader knows they must do: develop future leaders. Leadership, from personal leadership to that on a grander scale is about being of service, to those who you're guiding and developing. From your own experience, you understand that influence can be direct and indirect."

Alan nods as he speaks, "You indirectly impacted my career and life by your leadership skills and style with me. And I know others feel the same."

"We won't be around forever and those that will take our places need as much help and guidance as we can give them. The next generation wants and needs us to help them. If we don't coach, mentor and develop them ... there'll be chaos. They will model some form of leadership, thinking if it got them where they are, surely that's what they must continue to do. They will mimic others without fully understanding what leadership is or developing their own style. The detriment to that is, there will be a lot of robot leaders around.

"Leadership is an investment in others, when you take the time and resources to develop them or help them grow. Be of service to them.

"It's now your responsibility to help others step into the leaders they were meant to be. Help each of them uncover their own unique style of leadership. There is no one style; each of us brings our own strengths and special skills to leadership. Some of us are naturally gifted at big picture thinking, coaching, empowering others, strategy, developing teams etc.

"One other thing that I've notice in my years of coaching and developing others: female leaders have a different set of talents and gifts. Encourage women to embrace their feminine side. Use their femininity at the office instead of ignoring this side of them because they think being masculine will move them ahead quicker. I see too many women, and men, act like their male leadership role models, which are usually above them in the company hierarchy. I've heard many people share that they believed that style got their role model to higher positions, so it should work for them. Again, we each have unique talents and it's our responsibility as their coach and leader to help them see their uniqueness as a gift and not a hinder."

Jack pauses, to give Alan time to take in what he is hearing.

Alan takes a deep breath in and exhales before he speaks. "I can fully appreciate that. Wow. If I was admiring the wrong person and looking to them as a role model, I would really make some wrong assumptions about leadership and influencing others. We personally both know a number of people in leadership roles who should not be there. They've risen to the top in an unethical manner or they were promoted to become someone else's problem. Truthfully, you find those types of people in all industries."

"They're also not the type of people who will be sharing or developing others. It's a selfish way of being. I won't even call it leadership because it isn't. It's a self-serving way of being in charge."

"Yes, very self-serving," Alan nods "So, Jack, how would you suggest I develop a new generation of leaders?"

"Keep implementing all the other lessons I've shared with you. When you do, along with consciously being aware that you are developing them as a new generation of leaders, you will do great. Trust them, encourage them to stretch themselves, coach them instead of giving them the answers, respect their decisions, and best of all, let them fail."

"Let them fail? Shouldn't I stop mistakes before they happen?"

"Alan, yes, I would advise you to stop the big mistakes before they happen. Do this by coaching and helping them to see the various outcomes and different possibilities of their actions. Coaching helps people think and act differently. People learn more from their failures than successes. We celebrate our successes, and it ends there. When we fail, we tend to look at what went wrong, which is how we improve.

But the person who wants to constantly improve will reflect on the past project, meeting, investment, launch ... and ask themselves what could have been different and how can we improve it next time?

"As their leader, that is a skill you will need to develop for yourself and for your team. I call it *looking back to move forward*. Then you and your team will always be improving. Never be satisfied with where you are. Satisfaction never gets you loyalty. Someone, typically a competitor, will always beat you when you rest at 'be satisfied.' You want loyal customers, loyal clients, and loyal employees."

Alan, nods, and cocks his head to one side with a curious look on his face. "This is starting to sound like the final lesson."

"It is. It's time for us to part. Time for you to soar."

"Well, I really enjoy these meetings, to grow personally and professionally."

"I've given you several pieces of the puzzle, one of them being to never stop growing. But when you begin to teach these skills—or puzzle pieces—and lessons to others, you will begin to master them yourself with each new person you take under your wing and mentor."

They stand up, extending hands to shake one more time, this time in silence. The look of sincere gratitude is in Alan's eyes along with an eagerness to move forward as a leader.

"Thank you Jack, it's been a pleasure to learn from you again. I hope pr paths cross again and often."

"I'll be keeping an eye on you. You had something special when you worked with me in the beginning of your career. I knew you were a gold star then and you haven't disappointed me. You have more gifts and talents to share with others."

Alan watches Jack as he vanishes into the crowd of people. He opts to walk back to his office instead of taking a taxi.

## Questions:

- How are you investing in and developing others?

- How will you impact those around you?

- What kind of leader are you becoming?

*Coming together is a beginning;*
*keeping together is progress;*

*working together is success.*

**-Henry Ford**

# Chapter 12: A Walk in the Park

"Hi Mary ... yes, I'm fine ... okay, tell her I'll drop by her office this afternoon... Yes, drop by, as in 'in person.' I'll be back a little later than I expected.... Thank you, everything is good. Exceptional, actually."

The walk back to the office gives him some thinking time before returning. Time to reflect.

When is the last time he walked through the park? He doesn't have an answer.

Alan smiles and takes a deep breath of satisfaction with how far he's come.

*It was an investment. An investment of myself so I could then invest in others: my team, my company, my industry, my family. But an investment that paying off.*

Looking back on the skills and lessons his mentor has shared with him: developing relationships, getting to personally know others, listen, be fully present, focus, taking action on what you learn, being tenacious with new habits, not giving up on people too easily, hiring the right person for the culture based on their personality and not their resume and more.

He learned a few things about himself, like you really can teach an old dog new tricks. He chuckles to himself.

There was still more to do and become, but Alan is happy and so are his superiors with his progress. His boss doesn't know about these mentoring lunches. It is his secret, but others have noticed the change in him. Even his wife notices his stress level decreasing, and he's fully present when he's home with the family. Their marriage has grown stronger and the time and energy with the kids is worth the effort to adopt these new habits.

"Hmm," he thinks to himself, wondering how he will develop his team ever further to become stronger, more remarkable leaders.

He'd start by giving everyone a copy of the book Jack gave him. That should start the conversation. It is time to share with them what he's been learning; for them, the company, their clients, his family and oh yes, for himself. No investment in developing yourself is ever a waste, as long as you put into action what you learn. Being fully committed to serving others and assisting them to become the best version of themselves is the purpose.

*"Leadership is not what you do;
it's who you become."*
**-Laurie-Ann Murabito**


*Who are you becoming?*

# Additional Educational Resources

- Hire Laurie-Ann Murabito for a future meeting or event
  www.LaurieAnnMurabito.com/event-planners/

- Sign up for my brief weekly **FREE Leadership Tip** at:
  www.LaurieAnnMurabito.com

- Laurie-Ann's website has a number of free articles for you to
  download  www.LaurieAnnMurabito.com/articles/

- Follow me on Twitter at: www.twitter.com/LAMurabito

- Become a Facebook FAN at:
  www.facebook.com/pages/Laurie-Ann-Murabito

- Connect with me on LinkedIn at:        www.linkedin.com/in/
  laurieann

- Laurie-Ann's YouTube channel:
  www.youtube.com/user/LAMurabito

- Resources for purchase www.LaurieAnnMurabito.com

# Final Thoughts

I hope you've enjoyed this journey through leadership. This may be a story but I assure you, I've witnessed both personally and professionally, how a leader can change a team, an organization, and more. As I always say, *Leadership sets the tone.*

For additional resources, please visit LaurieAnnMurabito.com, where you can sign up for our newsletter and learn from the free resources available. Leaders continue to learn and this newsletter is designed with you in mind, the busy person.

***I'd love to hear from you!*** Please share your success stories, insights and ideas with me. Here's to your success and the remarkable leader that you are and are becoming.

Please go to Amazon, and leave a review. I appreciate your reviews and you'll be impacting others.

Support@LaurieAnnMurabito.com

LaurieAnnMurabito.com

# About the Author

*"Leadership is not what you do; it's who you become."*

Laurie-Ann Murabito is an award winning speaker and expert on high performance and leadership. Her book *Rethink Leadership,* was an Amazon Best Seller. She has several workbooks, such as *Blueprint for Success, Rethinking Leadership* and *HealthCARE Leadership.* Laurie-Ann's career began in healthcare, working in two different patient care departments, which couldn't have been more opposite. One worked as a team, with an engaged staff while the other was cut throat and only out for one's own interest. This experience changed her and inspired her to study performance, human behaviors, leadership and the science of achievement. Today she speaks, trains and coaches individuals and organizations wanting to achieve a higher level of success and create a memorable and powerful impact, *<u>authentically!</u>*

# Rethink Leadership

## *4 Lessons To Make You Remarkable*

*"Laurie-Ann took a large topic and puts it in a simple framework that anyone can apply ."*

**L. Fitzgerald**

*"Profound. Powerful. Motivating."* **A. Merchant**

A modern day parable about true inner leadership. It stars with you. A chance meeting in a coffee shop, starts four weeks of lessons that build on each other.

### You will learn how to:
- Start leading yourself before you can lead others
- Live an A+ life

Cultivate true and long lasting relationships

Lead without a title

Serve others while you lead

Develop future leaders

And much more....

www.ingramcontent.com/pod-product-compliance
Lightning Source LLC
Chambersburg PA
CBHW070029210526
45170CB00012B/510